T0196885

on
the tidings
of time

die gezeiten der zeit

poems
by
ralph günther mohnnau

english
christopher martin

Order this book online at www.trafford.com
or email orders@trafford.com

Most Trafford titles are also available at major online book retailers.

Print information available on the last page.

ISBN: 978-1-4120-6717-1 (sc)
ISBN: 978-1-4122-0802-4 (e)

Trafford rev. 05/28/2020

 www.trafford.com
North America & international
toll-free: 1 888 232 4444 (USA & Canada)
fax: 812 355 4082

Time…

Nearly twenty years have passed since I first encountered the enigmatic Ralph Günther Mohnnau.

In 1986, theatre colleague Manuel Lütgenhorst handed me a play in need of translating. Maybe you won't like it, he said. It's poetic, even pornographic, and very German. I was intrigued. ZEIT DER MUSCHELN (Time of the Conch) was poetic, yes, and erotic, and certainly more than peculiarly German. Yes, I said. CRY OF THE MANTIS — in collaboration with Daniel Woker — was the result.

Daniel returned to Switzerland shortly thereafter to be married and pursue his diplomatic career, and the day after the wedding I crossed into Germany to meet the mysterious Mohnnau for the first time. It was the beginning of a beautiful friendship, and our paths frequently crossed over the years in Paris, Berlin, Ibiza, or his native Frankfurt. As my own German improved, Mohnnau entrusted me with his earlier poems, collected in a companion volume: SOWING NIGHTSHADE IN THE WASTELANDS OF CITIES.

Time and tide…

In the course of the past two decades, Mohnnau has expanded his creative pursuits as a novelist and librettist for several major new operas; I have gone from directing the classics exclusively in New York to mounting productions for State and National Theatres in Europe and beyond; and Daniel Woker has become the Swiss Ambassador to Singapore.

On the tidings of time…

The ebb and flow took me this past year to Singapore to perform my version of Friedrich Dürrenmatt's MINOTAUR at a festival in the late playwright's honor initiated by Dan and his wife Myriam; and upon the returning tide, these latest Mohnnau poems on the subject of Time lay waiting.

After compiling the edition of his earlier poems, we decided this time around to include the German text on each facing page for comparison. This collection, *DIE GEZEITEN DER ZEIT*, can be read as a sometimes melancholy, sometimes intellectual, yet often ironic reflection on a theme that all of us studiously avoid until that moment in life when forced to stop and take stock of where we are, where we've been, and where we are ultimately headed—glimpses into the past, the present, and the future by a fascinating poet, at once fearless and yet fearful of his own journey *ON THE TIDINGS OF TIME*.

I urge you to take time and hearken to these tidings of great joy, of sorrow, of life itself...according to Ralph Günther Mohnnau.

Christopher Martin
New York, November 2005

cover photo
Gudrun Vékony

author photo
Jörg Poppe-Marquardt

german consultant
Pamela Curzon

on the tidings of time is published with a companion collection, *sowing nightshade in the wastelands of cities* — also available from Trafford Publishing.

the past shackles us
the present consumes us
the future beckons us

I

...*and thus hailed:*
       a life steeped in time

___*rgm*_____

der eisenbieger

als man den eisenbieger fragte
was die zeit sei
nahm er ein stück eisen
und bog es zu einem kreis
mit bloßen händen
das hier
sagte er
das ist die zeit

the iron-bender

as one asked the iron-bender
what time be
he took a piece of iron
and with his bare hands
bent it into a hoop
this here
said he
this is time

welche farbe hat die zeit?

ist sie blau?
ist sie gelb?
ist sie rot?

blau ist sie blau
wasserblau
　　　/
　　　　　lilienblau
　　　　　　　/
　　　　　　　　　tintenfischblau

rot ist sie rot
klatschmohnrot
　　　　/
　　　　　　lavarot
　　　　　　　/
　　　　　　　　　schamlippenrot

gelb ist sie gelb
des sommers
wenn sie tanzt
mit dem pinsel van goghs
über sonnenblumenfelder
&
zwischen
　　　taumelnden
　　　　　　sternen

what is the color of time?

is it blue?
is it yellow?
is it red?

blue is she blue
water-blue
              /
                  lily-blue
                         /
                             cuttlefish-blue

red is she red
wild poppy-red
                  /
                      lava-red
                           /
                               vulva-lip red

yellow is she yellow
of summer
when she dances
with the brush of van gogh
across the sunflower-meadows
&
among
        the tumbling
                      of stars

prometheus

licht begehrend
    & wärme
stahl ich
das feuer
den göttern

der ewigkeit zu entfliehen suchend
raubte ich ihnen
die zeit

so feuer
so zeit

schuf ich die menschen
nach meinem bilde
&
schuf auch: dich

prometheus

light desiring
    & warmth
I stole
the fire
of the gods

seeking to flee from eternity
I robbed them
of time

so fire
so time

creating I man
in my own image
&
so creating: thee

die zeit erzeugt eins

die zeit erzeugt eins
die zeit erzeugt zwei
die zeit erzeugt die
zehntausend spiegelungen
der welt

die zeit lehrt mich vieles:
sie lehrt mein aug
sie lehrt meine hände
sie lehrt meinen mund
sie lehrt mein ohr
sie lehrt meinen schatten
mein licht
mein hier - mein jetzt

mein niemals wieder

time begets one

time begets one
time begets two
time begets thus
ten thousand reflections of
the world

time teaches so much:
it teaches my eye
it teaches my hands
it teaches my mouth
it teaches my ear
it teaches my shadow
my light
my here – my now

my never again

ein mönch ging zum meister

ein mönch ging zum meister
und fragte ihn:
"was ist die zeit ?"
der meister sagte:
"nimm eine schere
und schneide sie in stücke"

nach einer weile
kam der mönch zurück
"meister
ich habe die jahre in tage geschnitten
die tage in stunden
die stunden
in minuten
die minuten in sekunden
und diese in immer kleinere stücke
ich finde kein ende"

da sagte der meister:
"fragtest du mich nicht
was die zeit sei?"

a monk went to his master

a monk went to his master
and asked of him:
"what is time?"
the master answered:
"take a pair of shears
and snip it into pieces"

after awhile
the monk returned
"master
I have snipped the years into days
the days into hours
the hours
into minutes
the minutes into seconds
and these in ever smaller pieces
still I find no end"

said the master:
"asked you not of me:
what is time?"

aus der hand frisst mir die zeit

aus der hand frisst mir die zeit:
wir sind freunde
sie begleitet mich
durch den morgen den mittag den abend
durch nächte und traum

wir spielen
wir tanzen
quecksilberspiele/feuertänze

sie schenkt mir pinsel und farbe
und sagt:
mache den himmel sonnenrot

sie schenkt mir einen korb voller worte
und sagt:
mache gedichte daraus
gelbe gedichte nicht wahr?

sie schenkt mir einen krug wasser
und sagt:
mache daraus ein meer
silberblau
voll mit leuchtendem plankton

sie nimmt mich unter ihre flügel
und sagt:
ich mache jetzt mit dir
eine reise zur ewigkeit
wir sammeln menschenseelen ein
und wenn wir zurückkommen
in sieben millionen jahren
wenn die erde verglüht ist
setzen wir sie aus
auf einem anderen planeten

time eats out of my hand

time eats out of my hand:
we're friends
she accompanies me
by morning noon and night
by sleep and dream

we play
we dance
quicksilver games/fire-dances

she gives me a brush and colors
and says:
turn the heavens sunshine-red

she gives me a basketful of words
and says:
turn these into poems
golden poems of course!

she gives me a jugful of water
and says:
turn this into a sea
silver-blue
filled with luminous life

she takes me under her wing
and says:
together we'll make
a voyage to eternity
we'll gather the souls of men
and when we return again
in seven million years
when the earth has burned to ash
we'll settle them
upon another of the planets

was aber ist die zeit?

sie blutet nicht
sie wirft keinen schatten
keinen anfang hat sie
&
kein ende
sie lässt sich nicht fangen
/
       nicht fesseln
/
        nicht küssen

sie kennt keine uhr

sie ist der leere krug
der darauf wartet
dass du ihn füllst

      mit deiner zeit

but what is time?

she bleeds not
she casts no shadow
no beginning has she
&
no end
she will not be seized
                    /
                        nor shackled
                                /
                                    nor embraced

she knows no clock

she the empty vessel
that waits upon
but you to fill her

                        with your time

sprechen wir von der zeit

sprechen wir von der zeit
denn kostbar ist sie
köstlicher als birne und aug

sprechen wir von der zeit
als wüchse sie dir aus der hand
wie junger mohn

sprechen wir von der zeit
als wäre sie eine muschel
und du die perle
die sich in ihr regt

sprechen wir von der zeit
wie von einem spiegel
durch den du hindurchgehst
wie durch einen wind:
nichts spürst du

sprechen wir von der zeit
wie von einer spur im sand:
auch wenn sie verweht
so ist sie doch gewesen

sprechen wir von der zeit
wie von einem licht
das dich unter seine flügel nimmt:
sie lehrt dich fliegen

let us speak of time

let us speak of time
for precious is she
precious more than apple and eye

let us speak of time
as if she sprouted from your hand
like a poppy-seed

let us speak of time
as if she were an oyster
and you the pearl
that stirs within

let us speak of time
as of a looking-glass
through which you step through
as through a wind:
sensing naught

let us speak of time
as of a print in the sand:
that when blown away
so still has been

let us speak of time
as of a light
that takes you under its wing:
and teaches you to fly

sprechen wir von der zeit
wie von einem wurfholz
das du in die luft schleuderst
wie weit
wie weit
und das zurückkehrt in deine hand
lautlos

sprechen wir von der zeit
wie von einem stein
der zu blühen beginnt

sprechen wir von der zeit
wie von einem feuer
das schon da war
bevor es dich gab
und das noch sein wird
wenn du nicht mehr bist

let us speak of time
as of a boomerang
you sling through the air
as far
as far
and that soundlessly comes back
in hand

let us speak of time
as of a stone
that begins to bloom

let us speak of time
as of a fire
already there
before there was you
and still will be
when you're no more

die zeit spricht

wenn jemand neben dir geht
& gleichzeitig siehst du ihn
auf einem hügel
eine halbe meile weit weg

wenn du im fluss schwimmst
& gleichzeitig fließt er
in den wolken über dir
& du mittendrin

wenn du am fenster stehst
& draußen spielt ein kind
& du erkennst:
das kind bist du selbst
VOR einem halben jahrhundert

dann träumst du nicht
gaukeln dir deine sinne nichts vor

dann weißt du nur:
du bist in mir
&
ich in dir

time speaks

when one beside you walks
& at the same time you see him
high upon a hill
a half a league away

when you the river swim
& at the same time it courses
in the clouds above your head
& you within its midst

when you at the window stand
& without there plays a child
& you recognize:
that child is you yourself
a half a century AGO

then dream you not
your wits do not deceive you

know this alone:
you are in me
&
I in you

von den sieben zuständen der zeit

ich griff in die zeit
siehe:
feucht war sie
wie lehm

ich trank die zeit
siehe:
salzig war sie
wie eine muschel

ich tanzte mit der zeit
siehe:
sie wirbelte mich
durch die lüfte

ich atmete die zeit
siehe:
fiebrig wurde mein blut

ich fesselte die zeit
siehe:
sie lacht über meine fessel

ich singe der zeit ein lied
siehe:
sie singt mit mir

ich küsse die zeit
siehe:
sie küsst mich zurück
mit offenen lippen

on the seven stages of time

I grasped at time
and see:
moist it was
as clay

I drank of time
and see:
salty was it
as an oyster

I danced with time
and see:
she whirled me
through the air

I breathed in time
and see:
fevered grew my blood

I shackled time
and see:
she scoffed away my bonds

I sing time a song
and see:
she sings with me

I time embrace
and see:
she embraces me in turn
lips open wide

die zeit und ich

sind eins
gemeinsam stehen wir am morgen auf
essen denselben apfel
trinken denselben tee
lesen dieselbe zeitung
gemeinsam gehen wir zur arbeit
fahren u-bahn in demselben zug
entblättern gemeinsam den tag
stunde um stunde
wie eine apfelsine

ein stiller begleiter ist mir die zeit
wo immer ich bin
auch in der liebe ist sie bei mir

doch dann & wann
lässt mich die zeit allein
des nachts zum beispiel
wenn alpträume mich heimsuchen/
            wenn schwarze vögel auf mich stürzen
wenn ich nicht weiß
wo ich bin & wer
ich in abgründe falle
zeitentrissen --

time and I

we're one
together rising in the morning
eating the same apple
drinking the same tea
reading the same paper
going off to work together
riding the same subway car
together peeling away the day
hour after hour
like an orange

a silent companion is my time
wherever I go
even when I love she's by my side

yet here & there
she leaves me time alone
at night for instance
when nightmares swell to haunt me/
              when the dark birds swoop upon me
when I know not
who & where I am
and fall into the void
untimely ripped --

                    BIS
sich die zeit wieder einstellt
sanft & plötzlich
wie ein sonnenstrahl
der durch den nebel bricht

dann tun wir so
die zeit & ich
als sei nichts gewesen
& gemeinsam lesen
wir ein gedicht

von sappho

TILL
time turns up again
soft & sudden
as a shaft of sunlight
bursting through the haze

and we make believe
my time & I
as if nothing's passed
& together we
read a poem

of sappho

du sagst

die zeit zerrinnt dir
unter deinen händen

IRRTUM

du zerrinnst
in den händen
der zeit

you say

time trickles
through your fingers

WRONG

you trickle
through the fingers
of time

der gott des skorpions

in der GROSSEN WÜSTE -- LE GRAND ERG
halte ich den geländewagen an
bei bordj el khadra
einem verlassenen fleck
in der verlassensten einöde

nichts als sand/steine/verbrannte erde: fels
einige trockendisteln
kriechen über den boden
wie schorf

die wüste ringsum:
ein glutofen
der sich ins nichts wölbt
                    lautlos zittert die luft

karim
mein führer
breitet seinen gebetsteppich aus
kniet nieder/verneigt sich in richtung mekka
ALLAHU AKBAR/ALLAH IST GROSS
höre ich ihn murmeln
selbstversunken

in meiner brusttasche knistert ein brief
meiner mutter aus deutschland
sie wünscht mir frohe ostern
im kirchenchor
schreibt sie
habe sie gesungen und vor vollen bänken
CHRIST IST ERSTANDEN

the god of scorpions

in the GREAT DESERT--LE GRAND ERG
I stopped the land rover
at bordj el khadra
a forsaken speck
of the most forsaken wasteland

nothing but sand/stone/scorched earth: rock
a few dried thistles
creeping across the ground
like scurf

the desert surround:
a scorching oven
vaulting away into the void
                              air quivering silently

karim
my guide
spreads his prayer rug out
kneels down/bows in the direction of mecca
ALLAHU AKBAR/ALLAH IS GREAT
I hear him murmur
self-absorbed

in my breast pocket a letter crackles
my mother in germany
wishing me a happy easter
in church choir
she writes
she sang before a packed house
CHRIST IS RISEN

uwe
mein freund aus alten & neuen tagen
lehnt am wagen
in seinem buddhistischen gewand
er starrt in die ferne
irgendwo ins nirgendwo

ZWEI MÖNCHE BETRACHTETEN EINE FAHNE / DIE ÜBER
DEM KLOSTERTOR FLATTERTE / DER WIND BEWEGT DIE
FAHNE / SAGTE DER EINE / NICHT DER WIND BEWEGT
DIE FAHNE / DIE FAHNE BEWEGT DEN WIND / SAGTE
DER ANDERE / SIE FRAGTEN DEN MEISTER / WER RECHT
HABE / WEDER BEWEGT DER WIND DIE FAHNE / NOCH
BEWEGT DIE FAHNE DEN WIND / EURE HERZEN
BEWEGEN SICH

ich schaue hoch in den himmel
in die sonne
wie ein schneidbrenner frisst sie sich durch das mehlige grau
an ihn
ECHNATON muß ich denken
den ketzerkönig der 18. dynastie
hier/in der großen wüste zwischen
dem 31. breiten- und 9. längengrad

O DU EINZIGER GOTT / ATON / DU ERFÜLLST JEDES
LAND MIT DEINER SCHÖNHEIT / SCHÖN BIST DU /
GROSS UND FUNKELND / DU BIST HOCH ÜBER DER
WELT / DEINE STRAHLEN UMARMEN ALLES / WAS DU
GEMACHT HAST / DIE TIERE / DIE MENSCHEN / DIE
ERDE / DAS LICHT UND DIE ZEIT / DU FESSELST SIE
DURCH DEINE LIEBE

uwe
my friend from past & present days
leans on the rover
dressed in his buddhist robes
staring into the distance
somewhere into nowhere

TWO MONKS REFLECTED ON A BANNER / FLUTTERING
ABOVE THE CLOISTER GATE / THE WIND STIRS THE
BANNER / SAID THE FIRST / THE WIND STIRS NOT THE
BANNER / THE BANNER STIRS THE WIND / SAID THE
OTHER / THEY ASKED OF THE MASTER / WHO WAS
RIGHT / NEITHER THE WIND STIRS THE BANNER / NOR
THE BANNER STIRS THE WIND / YOUR HEARTS ARE
STIRRING YOU

I look up at the sky
at the sun
tearing like an acetylene torch through the pasty gray
of him
AKHENATEN must I think
the heretic king of the 18th dynasty
here/in the great desert between
the 31st latitude and 9th longitude

O THOU ONLY GOD / ATEN / THOU GRACEST EVERY
LAND WITH THY LOVELINESS / LOVELY ART THOU /
GREAT AND GLITTERING / HIGH ART THOU ABOVE THE
WORLD / THY RAYS EMBRACING ALL / ALL THOU HAST
CREATED / THE BEASTS / MANKIND / THE EARTH / THE
LIGHT AND TIME / AND THOU BIND'ST THEM THROUGH
THY LOVE

ich schnicke mit dem fuß
einen stein zur seite
ein skorpion ist darunter/drohend richtet er seinen stachel auf
flüchtet in die nächste felsspalte

irgendwie
kriege ich das alles nicht zusammen
ALLAH / CHRISTUS / BUDDHA / ATON / SKORPION

wie auch immer:
jeder hat seinen eigenen gott

selbst
der skorpion

I flick a stone aside
with my foot
a scorpion lies beneath/threatened he thrusts his stinger out
fleeing into the nearest rocky crevice

somehow
I cannot reconcile it all together
ALLAH / CHRIST / BUDDHA / ATEN / SCORPION

whatever:
to each his own god

even
the scorpion

mein haus baue ich

mein haus baue ich
aus jahren/tagen & stunden
so wird es heißen: ein haus aus zeit

meine verse: ziegel & stein
meine träume: mörtel & stroh

mein leben keltere ich
aus augenblicken/honig & wein
so wird es heißen: ein leben trunken von zeit

wassergräben ziehe ich um mich
jahrhunderte tief

lasse die zugbrücke herunter

den zeitlosen

my house build I

my house build I
of years / of days & hours
and thus hailed: a house of time

my verses: of brick & stone
my dreams: of mortar & straw

my life will I press
of moments / honey & wine
and thus hailed: a life steeped in time

graven moats I'll have all round me
centuries deep

lower the drawbridge for

the timeless

von den tausend zeiten

tausend zeiten gibt es
und mehr

kennst du die zeit
des kleinen schweinemondes
oder die zeit
der kokosnussuhr
der wassermelonen
die zeit des stechginsters
der maulbeerblüten?

kennst du die zeit
der vier-winde
der vier-sonnen
oder
die zeit der perlmuscheln
die zeit des skorpions
die zeit des krokodils
die zeit der seepferdchen
die zeit der tanzenden flamingos?

of the thousand times

a thousand times there are
and more

know you the time
of the little pigs-in-the-moon
or the time
of the coconut-clock
of watermelons
the time of the prickly-pears
the mulberry-bush?

know you the time
of the four-winds
of the four-suns
or
the time of the pearl-oyster
the time of the scorpion
the time of the crocodile
the time of the seahorse
the time of the dancing flamingos?

eine feuchte zeit gibt es
        & eine trockene zeit
eine körnige zeit gibt es
        & eine flüssige zeit
eine klebrige zeit gibt es
        & eine schlüpfrige zeit
eine tanzende zeit gibt es
        & steinerne zeit
eine traumzeit gibt es
        & eine bahnhofsuhrzeit
eine gestauchte zeit gibt es
        & eine gedehnte zeit
eine männliche zeit gibt es
        & eine weibliche zeit
eine staubige zeit gibt es
        & eine sumpfige zeit
eine gekrümmte zeit gibt es
        & eine gerade zeit
eine wasserzeit
        & eine wüstenzeit
eine gefesselte zeit
        & eine chaoszeit

a humid time there is
        & a driest time
a granular time there is
        & a fluid time
a sticky time there is
        & a slippery time
a rocking time there is
        & a rocky time
a dreamtime there is
        & a train-departure time
a contracted time there is
        & an expanded time
a masculine time there is
        & a feminine time
a dusty time there is
        & a swampy time
a cyclical time there is
        & a linear time
a flooded time there is
        & a desert time
a shackled time there is
        & a chaos time

ja
auch das gibt es:
eine schamlose zeit
eine lüsterne zeit
eine geschredderte zeit
eine splitternde zeit
&
auch dies:
DEINE ZEIT

unbezähmbar ist die zeit

verzehrend sich in
diesem einzigen augenblick
um den
die götter
die ewigen
dich beneiden

yes
too there is:
a shameless time
a lascivious time
a shredded time
a splintered time
&
this too:
YOUR TIME

untamable is time

self-consuming in
this most precious moment
for this
the gods
the eternal
envy you

zeitenwende

manchmal
wechsle ich die zeit
wie ich die strassenseite wechsle

ich gehe hinüber in
eine andere zeit
wie durch einen spiegel

manche nennen es: tod
ich aber:
zeitenwende

time-bending

now and then
I change times
as I change sides of the street

and step across into
another time
as through a looking-glass

many call it: death
but I:
time-bending

kleine beschreibung der zeit

ohne körper ist sie
ohne form
messbar ist sie
aber nicht spürbar:
sie geht durch dich hindurch
wie ein röntgenstrahl: lautlos & unsichtbar

sie schlägt falten
sie krümmt sich
sie lässt sich strecken
                    /
                        stauchen
                                /
                                    streicheln

sie beherrscht die menschen
aber sie braucht keine gewalt

sie altert nicht

sie lässt sich nicht überlisten

sie lässt sich nicht spiegeln

die zeit ist die zeit ist die zeit

UND JETZT SPRICHT MR. SPOK:
die zeit ist das feuer
  in dem wir brennen

a brief description of time

without body is it
without form
measurable
but intangible:
it passes through you
as an x-ray passes through: silent & unseen

it carves wrinkles
it withers itself
it lets itself increase

        /

           contract

              /

                caress

it lords it over mankind
though it holds no sway

it ages not

it will not be outwitted

it will not brook reflection

time is time is time

AND NOW SAYS MR. SPOK:
*time is that flame
  in which we burn*

danke der zeit

danke der zeit
denn sie ist es
die dich am leben erhält
denn leben heißt: in der zeit sein

danke der zeit
denn sie lässt dich lieben
& küssen

danke der zeit
denn sie lehrt dich
dass du vergänglich bist

danke der zeit
so lange sie noch in dir ist
& du in ihr

danke der zeit
dass sie dich geschaffen hat

danke der zeit
weil sie dich begleiten wird
wie bald wie bald

in die zeitlosigkeit

thank time

thank time
for she it is
that lends you life
for life means: time to be

thank time
for she lets you love
& caress

thank time
for she teaches you
that you are fleeting

thank time
so long as she's in you
& you in her

thank time
that she's created you

thank time
for she'll accompany you
soon so soon

in timelessness

stell dir vor

stell dir vor
    die zeit sei der russ einer höhle
& du die hand
    die sich darin abbildet

stell dir vor
    die zeit sei ein wasserfall
& du das licht
    das sich zum regenbogen krümmt

stell dir vor
    die zeit sei eine säule aus stein
& du das salz
    das sie einstürzen lässt

stell dir vor
    die zeit sei ein roter fluss
& du ein gelbes blatt
    das auf ihm treibt

stell dir vor
    die zeit sei verbrannte erde
& du der regen
    der sie erblühen lässt

stell dir vor
    die zeit sei ein blitz
& du die hand
    die ihn auffängt

stell dir vor
    die zeit sei das feuer
& du die asche
    aus der du neu entstehst

imagine

imagine
    time to be the soot of caves
& you the hand
    that lives imprinted in it

imagine
    time to be a waterfall
& you the light
    that bends itself in rainbow

imagine
    time to be a pillar of stone
& you the salt
    that sends it crumbling

imagine
    time to be a crimson river
& you a yellowed leaf
    that drifts upon it

imagine
    time to be the barren earth
& you the rain
    that lets it blossom

imagine
    time to be a lightning bolt
& you the hand
    that catches it

imagine
    time to be that fire
& you the ash
    from which you rise anew

der gesang der zeit

ich bin es
    der das licht aussät
                über dem morgen
ich bin es
    der die steine sprechen lehrt
                des mittags
ich bin es
    der dein auge sehen lässt
                in der nacht
ich bin es
  der mit den winden zieht
                & die wasser aufwühlt
ich bin es
    der die wale singen lässt
                in den tiefen des meeres

ich bin der schatten
der über das schilf huscht
                & sich im sonnenlicht verliert
ich bin es
der das büffelgras wachsen lässt
                & das kind im schoss der mutter

ich bin es
    der in dir atmet

ich bin das auge des alls
das dich begleitet
durch deine tausend leben

the song of time

I am that
  which sows the light
                    across the morn
I am that
  which teaches stones to speak
                        at noon
I am that
  which lets your eyes see
                  in the night
I am that
  which rises with the winds
               & stirs the waters up
I am that
  which lets whales sing
          in the depths of the sea

I am that shadow
  which flits across the reeds
             & then is lost in sunlight
I am that
  which lets buffalo-grass sprout
         & the child in its mother's womb

I am that
  which breathes in you

I am that all-seeing eye
which accompanies you
throughout your thousand lives

bedenke dies o mensch

bedenke dies o mensch:
ein nichts ist die zeit vor der ewigkeit
eine ewigkeit ist sie vor dem nichts

die zeit die vergangen
sie ist dahin dahin
die zeit die da kommt
wer weiß wer weiß

bewahre dir die zeit
die durch dein herz fliegt:
diesen köstlichen
unwiederbringlichen
einzigen

augenblick

niemand
kann ihn dir nehmen
nicht einmal
GOTT

bethink this o man

bethink this o man:
a nil that time before eternity
an eternity that before the nil

time that is bygone
is past is past
time the still-to-come
who knows who knows

hold fast to time
as it flies through your heart:
this precious
this irretrievable
unique

blink of an eye

no one
can take that from you
not even
GOD

als seine schüler LAOTSE fragten
was sie im leben bedenken sollten

erkenne das licht
aber bewahre das dunkle
erkenne das männliche
aber bewahre das weibliche
erkenne die wahrheit
aber bewahre den irrtum
erkenne das leichte
aber bewahre das schwere
erkenne die stille
aber bewahre die unruhe
erkenne den himmel
aber bewahre den abgrund
erkenne das feuer
aber bewahre das wasser
erkenne das schweigen
aber bewahre das wort
erkenne das göttliche
aber bewahre das menschliche
erkenne das all
aber bewahre das nichts
erkenne dich selbst
aber bewahre das andere
erkenne die ewigkeit
aber bewahre die zeit
erkenne die liebe
und bewahre sie dir

when his students asked LAOTSE
what they should think upon in life

know the light
but embrace the dark
know the masculine
but embrace the feminine
know the truth
but embrace the error
know the simple
but embrace the hard
know you peace
but embrace unrest
know you heaven
but embrace the void
know you fire
but embrace you water
know you silence
but embrace the word
know the godly
but embrace the human
know the universe
but embrace the nil
know thyself
but embrace the other
know eternity
but embrace you time
know you love
and she embrace

zu fragen

zu fragen:
was war vor der zeit
ist wie zu fragen: wo war ich
bevor ich geboren
wurde

es ist die zeit
in der du einst warst
bevor du geworfen wurdest

in diese zeit

to question

to question:
what was before time was
is as to question: where was I
before I was born
to be

it is that time
in which you once were
before you were thrust into

this time

abend bei bordj el khadra

in den zelten längst
ist es still geworden
die kamele liegen
wie steinerne schatten
gegen den horizont

opal das schweigen des himmels

nichts hörst du
selbst die sterne
sind stumm
&
stumm auch ist die zeit

die ihre netze eingeholt hat
gefüllt
mit der beute
des tages

nightfall at bordj el khadra

in tents long since
has all grown still
camels crouched
like stony shadows
against the horizon

opal the silence of the heavens

not a sound
even the stars
are silent
&
silent too is time

which has drawn in its nets
chock-full
with the catch
of the day

der fluss

über's gebirg
will ich fließen
in's tal

sagte der fluss

die wolken lächelten
das
schaffst du nie

der fluss
nahm sich zeit

zehn millionen jahre

siehe
jetzt fließt er in's meer
sprudelnd
durch den schnitt
im gebirg

the stream

over the rock
to the glen
I'd run

said the stream

the clouds above smiled
never
come to pass

the stream
took its time

ten million years

look
now it runs to the sea
tumbling
through the pass
in the rock

zeit & zen

es wird eine zeit geben
               nach der zeit
wie es eine zeit gegeben hat
               vor der zeit

aber diese zeit wird nicht
mehr dieselbe sein
keinen anfang haben wird sie
&
kein ende

sie wird sich nicht biegen lassen
&
nicht vergehen

sie wird sein
wie der ton der bambusflöte
in der abenddämmerung
der über den see streicht
   und sich verliert

im zeitlosen

now & zen

there will come a time
                          beyond time
as there was once a time
                          before time

but this time will not
be of the same
it shall have no beginning
&
no end

it will not allow itself to bend
&
not be passed

it will come
as the sound of the bamboo flute
in the autumnal twilight
stretching far across the lake
   to fall away

in timelessness

lebenszeit : zeitlebens

geboren wirst du
aus der zeit
sterben wirst du
in der zeit

dein leben:

verweilen
zwischen zeiten

lifetime : timelife

born were you
out of time
die shall you
within time

your life:

meantime
between times

II

...that is time
   spilling across your tongue

_____*rgm*_____

lege dein ohr

lege dein ohr
an einen hohlen kürbis
und lausche seinem klang:
du hörst die zeit

presse die zitrone
in deinem mund:
es ist die zeit
die über deine zunge rollt

sei jener physiker
der das zerriebene gestein
eines meteoriten
über einem glasrohr erhitzte
bis sich dampf bildete
und als wasser herabtropfte
so alt wie das sonnensystem
viereinhalb milliarden jahre

dieses wasser
sagte er
ist flüssige zeit

lay your ear

lay your ear
to a hollow gourd
and listen to its sound:
it's time you hear

squeeze a lemon
in your mouth:
that's time
spilling across your tongue

to be the physicist
who ground the rock
of a meteorite
above his bunsen burner
till it turned to steam
and water trickled down the tube
as old as the solar system
four and a half billion years

this water
said he
is liquid time

kleine zeitketzerei

der anfang der zeit
war ein punkt
von unendlicher dichte
&
unendlicher krümmung der raumzeit
vor zehnmilliarden jahren

genannt auch: URKNALL/BIG BANG
                                    (so die wissenschaftler)
O KÖSTLICHER IRRTUM!

die zeit war einfach schon da
eine schleife ist sie
ohne anfang / ohne ende
drehend & spiegelnd sich
in schönstem bewusstsein
ihrer selbst

lachend vor sich hertreibend
den urknall
wie eine pusteblume
                        (so die dichter)

brief time heresy

the beginning of time
was a point
of infinite density
&
infinite bending of space/time
ten billion years ago

known as: URKNALL/BIG BANG
                                    (so the physicists)
O PRECIOUS ERROR!

time was simply there
a loop is she
without beginning / without end
twisting & admiring
the mirrored fairest of them all
herself

laughing to herself as she puffs
the big bang into being
like a dandelion
                            (so the poets)

frage der zeit an dich

tag um tag
isst & atmest du
milliarden atome

tag um tag
scheidest du aus
milliarden atome

ein neuer mensch bist du geworden
so nach jahren
ausgetauscht in der zeit
vollkommen & unwiederbringlich
nichts ist übrig geblieben
von dir
keine zelle
     /
       kein atom
         /
          NICHTS
was also ist es
das dich so sicher sein lässt

du seist noch immer
derselbe
wie vor zeiten?

questions time of you

day by day
you eat & breathe in
billions of atoms

day by day
you jettison off
billions of atoms

a new man have you become
following years
transformed through time
utterly & irretrievably
nothing at all left
of you
not a cell
            /
        an atom
                /
                    NIL
so what is it
that lets you be so certain

that you are still
the same
as in times past?

der atomphysiker und die zeit

wissen Sie
mein herr
was geschieht
wenn ich zwei lichtteilchen
im laser erzeuge
und sie gleichzeitig durch glasfasern
auf zwei spiegel lenke
halbdurchlässige spiegel?
Sie werden es nicht erraten:
die teilchen verhalten sich immer gleich
sie werden beide hindurchgelassen
oder beide zurückgeworfen
wie aneinander geketttete zwillinge
etwas anderes gibt es nicht
die teilchen rufen sich gegenseitig zu
jetzt gehen wir durch den spiegel
oder auch:
wir lassen uns zurückwerfen
sie sind verschränkt
wie wir atomphysiker sagen
Sie meinen
daran sei nichts besonderes?

time and the nuclear physicist

do you know
my friend
what happens
when I take a laser and generate
two particles of light
and simultaneously through fiberglass
train them on a pair of mirrors
semi-translucent mirrors?
you will never guess:
the reaction of the particles never varies
either both transmitted through
or both reflected back
as if they were a pair of siamese-twins
anything else impossible
the particles call out to one another
let's penetrate the mirror
or else:
let's be refracted back
irrefutably linked
as we physicists might say
you think
that that's not something special?

NUN

was glauben Sie
wie schnell sie sich
untereinander verständigen
das eine zu tun oder das andere?
staunen Sie:
zehn millionen mal schneller
als das licht
tja
der alte einstein hatte sich geirrt
als er sagte
in der natur sei nichts schneller
als das licht

der atomphysiker lächelt geheimnisvoll
das ist noch nicht alles
wenn ich jetzt ein teilchen
auf einen spiegel lenke
der sich sehr schnell fortbewegt
und gleichzeitig ein teilchen
auf einen stehenden spiegel
prallen lasse
mein herr
kitzeln Sie Ihr gehirn
was geschieht dann?
meinen Sie
das lichtteilchen
das auf den stehenden spiegel trifft
kommt früher an als dasjenige
das auf den schnellen spiegel prallt?

NOW

can you imagine
just how fast they
one another communicate
to go the one way or the other?
imagine it:
ten million times as fast
as light
tsk
old einstein himself had it wrong
when he said
in nature there is nothing faster
than light

the nuclear physicist smiled mysteriously
and that's not all
if I were now to take one particle
and direct it on a mirror
propelled at extreme high-speed
and simultaneously ricochet
a second off a mirror standing
stationary
just tickle your brain
my friend
what happens then?
you'd think
the particle of light
that strikes the stationary mirror
will arrive ahead of the other
ricocheting off the mirror at high-speed?

IRRTUM
mein herr

denn
glauben Sie's oder glauben Sie es nicht
nach der messung im zeitsystem
des fliehenden spiegels
trifft das teilchen früher auf
als das andere auf dem stehenden
spiegel
während bei dem stehenden spiegel
das teilchen ebenfalls als erstes aufprallt
was heißt:
staunen Sie staunen Sie
KEINES DER BEIDEN KOMMT
ALS ERSTES AN oder vielmehr:
beide kommen als erste an
was das gleiche ist
ALSO
sollte man meinen
sie können sich auch nicht
untereinander austauschen

WRONG
my friend

for
believe it or believe it not
by measuring the time-scheme
of the fleeing mirror
this particle strikes ahead
of the one off the mirror standing
stationary
whereas the particle also ricochets
upon and off the stationary mirror first
which means:
surprise surprise
NEITHER OF THE TWO
ARRIVES AHEAD or rather:
both of them arrive ahead
all things being equal
AND SO
one might suppose
that they're incapable
of being interchanged

                    ABER
halten Sie den atem an:
trotzdem haben sich die pärchen
wie im ersten versuch
untereinander verständigt
obwohl sie dazu
nach menschlichem ermessen
& den gesetzen von ursache und wirkung
gar keine zeit hatten
was heißt:
das eine teilchen weiß schon vorher
ehe es aufprallt
wie sich das andere teilchen verhält
sie verabreden sich untereinander
sozusagen im zeitlosen raum
und das
ob sie nun einen meter von einander entfernt sind
oder eine million lichtjahre
oder soll ich sagen:
für einen kurzen augenblick
steht die zeit still
ja die zeit steht still
ES GIBT SIE NICHT
                    /
                    ausgelöscht ist sie

aufgegangen in einer zeit
die wir nicht kennen
die ich meta-zeit nenne
das ist die zeit
die vorwärts wie rückwärts läuft
über uns hinweg
durch uns hindurch
oder auch stillsteht
            wie es ihr gefällt –

AH BUT

hold your breath now:
nevertheless these particles have
as in our first experiment
communicated to one another
albeit
given the measurements of man
& the laws governing cause and effect
there was not sufficient time
which means:
one of the particles knows in advance
before the ricochet
how the other particle will react
in cahoots with one another
so to speak in timeless space
as if
they were less than a meter from each other
or a million light years
or should we say:
for one split second
time stands still
oh yes time stands still
DOES NOT EXIST
                    /
                        erased is she

evaporating into a time
which we know not
which I'll call meta-time
that time which
is running backwards forwards
above beyond
and through us
or merely standing still
                        just as it likes –

gespenstisch
nicht wahr?
es gibt eine zeit jenseits der zeit
das ist es
was ich sagen will
ich verstehe das nicht
und
Sie verstehen das noch weniger
vergangenheit gegenwart und zukunft
darin hat einstein wiederum recht
ist eine
wenn auch
hartnäckige illusion

nehmen Sie also die welt
um sich herum
nicht so ernst
sie ist ein irrlichtender spuk
ein taumelndes trugbild
eine fata morgana
die eigentliche welt
aus der Sie in dieses leben
geworfen worden sind
und in die Sie zurückkehren werden
wenn der irdische tanz vorbei ist --
in ihr steht die zeit still
oder sollte ich sagen
sie ist die zeitlose welt
die welt jenseits des urknalls
aus der Ihre und meine zeit
nur abgespalten wurde --
was sind wir also mehr
als ein splitter der zeit?

spooky
isn't it?
that there's a time outside of time
one that
I'd have to say
even I don't comprehend
and
you'd comprehend still less
the past the present and the future
in this sense was einstein right
are an
illusion
if persistent illusion

so don't take the world
around you
so in earnest
she's a will-o'-the-wisp
a shimmering mirage
a fata morgana
and the intrinsic world
out of which in life
you shall be hurled
and into which return
when this earthly dance has passed --
time stands still for her
or should I say
she that timeless world
that world beyond big bang
from which your time and mine
has simply split away --
so what are we more
than a splinter of time?

gehen Sie jetzt nach hause
& trinken Sie einen doppelten whisky
auf die zeit
auf Ihre zeit
denn sie ist's
die Sie
begleitet in die

unsterblichkeit

so go on home now
& raise yourself a double whiskey
to time
your time
she the one
who will
accompany you into

immortality

der uhrmacher und die zeit

sehen Sie
sagte der uhrmacher
wenn ich das pendel der uhr anhalte
steht die zeit
z.b. ist es jetzt 17 h 23

auch nach einer stunde
oder nach zehn tagen
oder nach einem jahr
oder nach tausend jahren:

immer ist es 17 h 23

wenn ich danach das pendel
bewege
springt die zeit wieder an
nicht wahr?

jetzt ist es eine minute später
17 h 24
wie viele tage oder jahre auch verflossen sind seit
ich das pendel angehalten habe
der zeiger bewegt sich wieder
als hätte er nie still gestanden
die uhr läuft weiter
als sei die zeit nie stehen geblieben

time and the clockmaker

you see
said the clockmaker
if I stop the pendulum on this clock
time stands still
e.g. it is now 5:23 pm

and come an hour
or come ten days
or come a year
or come a thousand years:

it will still be 5:23 pm

if I set the pendulum
in motion
time continues to run
not so?

it's now a minute later
5:24 pm
how many days or years have passed since
I stopped the pendulum
the hand moves now
as if it had never stopped
the clock continues
as if time had never stood still

jenseits der uhr aber
ist die zeit weitergelaufen
& läuft einfach immer weiter
& weiter
doch diese zeit existiert
für die uhr nicht
verstehen Sie?

sowenig die zeit für Sie
existiert
die Sie im schlaf verbringen

und so ist es mit der zeit
vor Ihrer zeit
&
so wird es sein mit der zeit
nach Ihrer zeit
&
der zeit zwischen diesen beiden zeiten
sie existiert
&
sie existiert nicht
aber wer will das schon
entscheiden?
und erst wenn Sie träumen:

outside the clock however
time continues to run
& just keeps on running
& running
yet this time did not exist
within the clock
you follow me?

as little as time exists
for you
that you expend in sleep

and so it is with time
before your time
&
so it will be with time
beyond your time
&
time between these times
exists
&
or not
but who the one to
establish that?
and even in your dreams:

wenn die gesetze von ursache & wirkung
& der schwerkraft aufgehoben sind
wenn Sie sich in einen anderen
menschen verwandeln können oder
in eine klapperschlange oder
ihr geschlecht ändern
wenn sie durch zeit & raum fliegen
mit überlichtgeschwindigkeit zurück
zum urknall
   ODER
     bis ans ende des alls
wenn die vergangenheit zukunft wird
& die zukunft vergangenheit
& beide sich ineinanderschlingen
zu einer traumzeit jenseits der zeit
ich frage Sie:
welche zeit ist die eigentliche zeit?

der uhrmacher seufzt

die französischen revolutionäre
haben sich geirrt
als sie auf die turmuhren schossen
& glaubten
so die alte zeit abschaffen zu können
nachdem sie den könig geköpft hatten
die uhren blieben stehen
ja
aber die zeit lief einfach
über sie hinweg
selbst als sie die pendel
unter das fallbeil legten lief
sie weiter wie das wasser
eines flusses das
zum meer fliesst

when the laws of cause & effect
& the force of gravity are suspended
when you can turn yourself
into someone else or
to a rattlesnake or
change your sex
and soar through time & space
beyond the speed of light straight back
to the big bang
                    OR
                        to the end of all
when the past becomes the future
& future becomes the past
& they entwine with one another
in a dreamtime outside of time
I ask you:
which time then is actual time?

the clockmaker sighs

the french revolutionaries
were mistaken
when they fired at the tower-clocks
& believed
they'd abolish time as known
once the king had been beheaded
the clocks stood still
yes
but time just simply
passed them by
even as they lay the pendulum
beneath the guillotine it kept on
running like the water
of a stream that
runs to sea

und da ist noch
die ewigkeit -
wissen Sie
was die ewigkeit ist?
nein?
es ist das
was bleibt
wenn man die zeit
von ihr abzieht
sie häutet sozusagen
sie ist die zeitlose zeit
die sich vollendet hat
aber wer wollte schon
in einer solchen ewigkeit leben
steinern & tot
wie eine salzwüste?

was ich eigentlich sagen wollte:
leben Sie jetzt
diesen augenblick
Sie haben keinen anderen
aber hüten Sie sich davor
sich zu sehr mit der zeit
zu beschäftigen

sie wird Sie verschlingen

and there's still
eternity --
do you know
what this eternity is?
no?
it is what
is left
when one subtracts
her time away
or sheds it so to speak
and its sum total
timeless time
but who would wish
to live in such eternity
bleak & barren
as a salt-desert?

what I really meant to say is:
live now
in this moment
you have no other
and guard yourself against
being far too occupied
with time

or it will swallow you

der schlangenbeschwörer und die zeit

wenn ich auf meiner
flöte spiele
sehen Sie genau hin
sagt der schlangenbeschwörer
windet sich die schlange aus ihrem korb
wiegt sich im spiel meiner flöte
tanzt vor mir
bewegt ihren körper
im takt der musik
ganz wie ich will

wenn ich jetzt innehalte
sehen Sie
fällt die schlange wieder
in den korb zurück
reglos liegt sie da
versteinert ist sie
wie ausgestorben

er schaut mich
durchdringend an

time and the snake-charmer

when I play
my flute
watch closely now
says the snake-charmer
the snake unwinds from its basket
sways to the playing of my flute
dances there
moving her body
in time to the music
exactly as I wish

when I now stop playing
you see
the snake drops back again
into the basket
and lies motionless
as stone-cold there
as if in death

he darts me
a piercing look

genauso ist es
mit der zeit -
nur wenn du sie hervorlockst
mit dem spiel deiner flöte
deinem gesang
/
        deinen gedanken
erwacht sie aus ihrer starre
tanzt nach deiner melodie
wiegt sich in deinem takt
ist dir zu diensten
aber sie entschlüpft dir
wie eine glitschige eidechse
wenn du sie missachtest
das heilige in ihr
nicht erkennst

in seinen augen
glimmt etwas lauerndes
sphinxhaftes

wieder entlockt er
seiner flöte
einige töne
schwermütig
/
        verführerisch
/
            perlend wie tau
an einem bambusblatt
wie aus dem nichts
taucht sie wieder auf
die schlange
wiegt ihren kopf hin und her
ihren körper
zu den tönen der flöte
tanzt sie

and so it is
with time –
only when you lure her forth
with your flute
your song
            /
                your thoughts
you wake her from her stupor
she sways in time
dances to your tune
at your command
but she will slither away
like a slippery lizard
if you ignore her
or fail to recognize that
she is sacred

in his eyes
a glimmering hint
of the sphinx

he again elicits
from his flute
a tone
so sorrowful
            /
                seductive
                    /
                        pearling like dew
upon a bamboo leaf
out of nowhere
the snake
dives up again
head swaying to and fro
her body
dancing to the sound
of the flute

schwerelos
/
        wie in trance

sehen Sie
das ist es
was Sie lernen müssen
von der zeit
sagt der schlangenbeschwörer
ob sie bei Ihnen ist
oder nicht
ob sie Ihnen dient
oder nicht
hängt alleine von Ihnen ab

er lächelt und reicht mir seine flöte
spielen Sie
spielen Sie
ich schenke sie Ihnen
von nun an sind Sie
herr über die zeit
wie über die schlange
ABER
vergessen Sie nie
das heilige in ihr

unbekümmert wie ein kind
blase ich ein paar töne auf der flöte
blase einfach darauf los
laut
/
   ausgelassen
/
      schrill
/
          wie glasscherben
splittern die töne umher

weightless
/
     as in trance

you see
this is what
you need to learn
of time
says the snake-charmer
is she with you
is she not
does she obey you
does she not
it rests with you alone

he smiles and hands me his flute
play it
play it
it's yours I give it to you
from now on you
the master of time
as of the snake
BUT
never forget that
she is sacred

innocent as a child
I blow a few notes on the flute
let loose and blow
loud
/
   blasting
/
     shrill
/
       as glass-shards
splintering the air

DA
schießt die schlange aus dem korb hervor
zuckt wie unter stromschlägen
näher und näher kommt sie
mit gelben stechenden augen
die pupillen ein strich
starrt mich an
züngelt mit spitzer zunge
stößt auf mich zu -
dann wird es schwarz um mich herum

als ich wieder zu mir komme
sehe ich den schlangenbeschwörer
sehe wie er die schlange am hals hält
zwischen daumen und zeigefinger
spitz ragen die giftzähne
aus ihrem maul heraus
eine durchsichtige zähe flüssigkeit
schliert an ihnen herunter

NOW
springs the snake out of the basket
jolts as if by an electric shock
closer and closer she comes
with those yellow piercing eyes
pupils all a-slit
staring at me
that forked tongue thrusting
darting at me --
then all goes black around me

when I come to again
I can see the snake-charmer
can see he has the snake by the neck
between his thumb and forefinger
sharp venomous fangs
sticking from its jaws
a translucent gluey substance
oozing down from them

der schlangenbeschwörer nimmt einige tropfen
auf einen finger
steckt ihn in den mund
leckt das gift ab

Sie hatten verdammt glück
sagt er
was ich vergessen habe
Ihnen zu sagen:
spielen Sie niemals falsch oder
versuchen Sie die zeit zu überlisten

er zeigt auf die zähne
ein tropfen des schlangengifts genügt
um ein dutzend menschen umzubringen
wenn das gift in das blut kommt
dagegen gibt es kein
gegengift
Sie sind verloren
hoffnungslos
er lächelt geheimnisvoll
es sei denn
Sie schlucken das gift
hinunter
wie ich es getan habe
wenn Sie das schaffen
verliert die zeit
ihre schrecken
und Sie können von ihr sagen:

ich habe sie gezähmt

the snake-charmer takes one single drop
upon his finger
sticks it in his mouth
licks the venom off

damned lucky this time
he says
what I'd neglected
to tell you is:
never play a false note or
attempt to get the better of time

he points to the fangs
one drop of this snake-venom is enough
to bring the deaths of at least a dozen men
once the poison gets into the blood
and there's no
antidote
you'd be lost
utterly lost
he smiles knowingly
however
if you simply swallow
the venom
as I've just done
if you do that
then time will lose
its dread
and you can simply say:

I have tamed it

die sonne

verglühen wird sie
in viereinhalb milliarden jahren
aufblähen wird sie sich
zu einem roten riesen

versprühend
licht & feuer
feuer & licht
in die tiefe
des alls

erstrahlen wird sie
in schönheit
heller leuchten wird sie
als je zuvor

ehe sie in sich zusammenstürzt
unter dem gewicht
ihrer eigenen schwerkraft
endend als weisser zwerg

verbrennen mit ihr
werden die erde
die menschen
ihre lieder
ihre gebete

nur
die zeit
überlebt

lächelnd

the sun

she'll burn herself out
in four and a half billion years
   blowing herself up
      into a big red giant

spewing
light & fire
fire & light
into the depths
of the void

radiant oh yes
in loveliness
shining ever brighter
than before

then whithering she'll collapse
beneath the weight
of her own gravity
and end as a white dwarf

scorched along with her
will be the earth
and all mankind
its songs
its prayers

time
will alone
survive

smiling

über die gemeinsamkeiten von zeit & wasser

du kannst in sie eintauchen
du kannst dich von ihr tragen lassen
sie gleitet dir durch die hand
sie kann schweigen
sie tritt über das ufer
du kannst sie trinken
ja hast du die zeit je getrunken?
versuche es

sie fragt nicht:
wer bist du?
was ist dein name?
woher kommst du?
wer ist dein gott?

sie verdunstet:
ja die zeit verdunstet
wusstet du das nicht?

auch das ist sie:
nebel
        /
            regen
                /
                    wolken
                        /
                            schnee
der raureif über
den dächern am morgen
ebbe & flut

aus ihr entsteht alles leben

wasser & zeit:
dasselbe

you can dive into her
you can let yourself be swept away
she'll trickle through your fingers
she can be silent
overrun her banks
you can drink her
yes have you never drunk of time?
try it sometime

she asks not:
who art thou?
what thy name?
whither com'st thou?
who thy god?

she evaporates:
yes time evaporates
knew you not that?

and too is she:
fog
   /
     rain
       /
        clouds
           /
             snow
the frost upon
the rooftops in the morning
ebb & flow

from her all life begins

time & tide:
alike

Sie wissen mein herr

Sie wissen
mein herr:
die welt
so wie wir sie sehen
die gibt es nicht
auf die netzhaut wird sie geworfen
auf dem kopf stehend
sozusagen verkehrt herum
& doch gaukelt uns das gehirn vor
alles gehe mit rechten dingen zu:
die flasche stehe auf dem tisch
& nicht der tisch auf der flasche
der regen falle aus den wolken auf die erde
& nicht umgekehrt
die straßenbahn fahre von rechts nach links
& nicht von links nach rechts
jetzt frage ich Sie
mein herr:

you know my friend

you know
my friend:
the world
as we see her
doesn't exist
she is cast upon the retina
standing on her head
downside up one might say
& yet our brains trick us in believing
everything is just as it should be:
the vase stands on the table
& not the table on the vase
the rain falls from the clouds upon the earth
& not the opposite
the streetcars travel from right to left
& not from left to right
now let me ask
my friend:

was wäre
wenn das gehirn uns noch andere dinge vorspiegelte?
zum beispiel dass die zeit immer geradeaus läuft
während sie doch in wirklichkeit
sich rückwärts bewegt oder im kreis herum?
dass die träume wahr sind & das leben ein traum?
dass wenn die traumzeit sich verbindet mit
der irdischen zeit
sie sich auslöschen gegenseitig
wie minus und plus
& von Ihnen
& mir
nichts übrig bleibt

nicht einmal
der schatten
eines sandkorns
in der sahara ?

what if
our brains managed to invert still other things?
that time for example runs straight on
whereas in reality
it runs in reverse or in a loop?
that dreams are real & life a dream?
that if our dreamtime is linked with
earthly time
they ought to cancel one another out
like plus and minus
& of you
& me
nothing remains

not even
the shadow
of a grain of sand
in the sahara?

ich warf das netz aus

ich warf das netz aus
und siehe:
die zeit hatte ich gefangen
sie zappelte darin
wie eine fledermaus
stieß spitze schreie aus

eine weile betrachtete ich sie
wie sie ängstlich umherflatterte
mit ihren durchsichtigen flügeln
mit ihren fiebrigen augen
den spitzen ohren

endlich
ließ ich sie
frei

I cast out my net

I cast out my net
and see:
it was time I'd snagged
struggling there
like a bat shrieks
screeching to get out

for a while I kept an eye on her
as she anxiously fluttered about
with her translucent wings
with her feverish eyes
her pointed ears

in the end
I set her
free

zeit(w)ende

nach all den millionsten und milliardsten sekunden
nach immer winzigeren nanosekunden /
pikosekunden / femto-sekunden
die planck-zeit:
das ende der messbaren zeit

sie zerfällt zu staub & asche
wie du
&
ich
wie das lachen
&
der schrei der möwen
der glockenschlag
das echo über dem see
das hämmern des pressluftbohrers
das zirpen der zikaden
nichts bleibt
als eine
steinerne
stille –
                    DOCH DANN
erblüht sie wieder
zu neuer zeit
zu neuem lachen
&
lieben
zu neuem glockenschlag
&
zikadenzirpen
wie die wüste
neu erblüht
bei regen nach tausend jahren
trockenheit

time(b)end

after all the millionths and billionths of seconds
after the ever-diminutive nano-seconds /
pico-seconds / femto-seconds
comes planck-time:
the end of measurable time

ashes to ashes & dust to dust
like you
&
me
like laughter
&
the cry of seagulls
the striking of a clock
the echo across the lake
the pounding of jackhammers
the chirping of crickets
nothing left
but a
stone-cold
silence –
                              YET THEN
she blossoms again
in time anew
in laughter anew
&
in love
new strikings of the clock
&
crickets chirping
as the desert
blossoms anew
in raining after a thousand years
of drought

rätsel

das licht der sonne
benötigt 8 minuten und 18 sekunden
bis zur erde –

wie lange
braucht für die gleiche strecke
die zeit?

riddle

the light of the sun
requires 8 minutes and 18 seconds
to reach the earth --

how long
to travel the same distance
for time?

zeitenlauf

man muss der zeit
zeit geben

wie man
dem stein zeit geben muss
zu blühen
&
dem fluss die zeit
zurückzukehren
zu seiner quelle

time-run

one must give the time
to time

as one
must give a stone the time
to bloom
&
the stream the time
to return again
to its source

III

...out of the lap of my beloved

lapping time

___*rgm*_____

setz dich auf einen fels

setz dich auf einen fels
am meer
lausche seinen wellen:

soviel kann es dir erzählen
von menschen
von ihrer zeit
von kommen
von vergehen

von wracks
die zerfallen auf seinem grund

von leben
das aus ihm entstanden

von der zeit die war
als es noch keine zeit gab

von der zeit die sein wird
wenn es keine zeit mehr gibt

in seiner tiefe bewahrt das meer
die geschichte der menschen
& ihrer zeit

& auch die geschichte
von dir & von mir
& unserer liebe

sit high upon a cliff

sit high upon a cliff
above the sea
and listen to its swell:

so much does it have to tell
of men
their time
their rise
their fall

of wrecks
once dashed upon its shoals

of life
from out its waves has sprung

of a time that was
as if there were no time to be

of a time to come
when there be time no more

in the depths of the sea there lies
the history of man
& his time

& so the history
of you & me
& of our love

für g.

die zeit
die du in dir trägst
ist eine andere zeit
als die
die ich in mir trage

die wieder
andere zeiten sind
als die
in der wir beide
schwimmen
in diesem
köstlichen
augenblick

wenn wir uns
lieben

for g.

the time
you bear in you
is yet another time
than that
I bear in me

then again
still other times
as those
in which we swim
as one
in this
most precious
moment

when we two
love

ins haar meiner liebsten

ins haar meiner liebsten
flechte ich die zeit:
nicht mehr entschlüpft sie mir

unter die zunge meiner liebsten
träufle ich die zeit:
geschmeidig wird sie
wie eine eidechse

aus dem schoss meiner liebsten
trinke ich die zeit:
ein dürstender bin ich
nach der zeit

im auge meiner liebsten
lockt die zeit:
lass uns lieben

zeit
&
zeitenlos

in the hair of my beloved

in the hair of my beloved
plaiting time:
so she'll not escape me

upon the tongue of my beloved
trickling time:
that she'll be supple
as a lizard

out of the lap of my beloved
lapping time:
an awful thirster am I
after time

in the eye of my beloved
urges time:
let us love

time
&
timeless

zertrümmert liegt die zeit

zertrümmert liegt die zeit:
es ist nicht an dir und mir
die scherben aufzulesen noch
sie wieder zusammenzufügen

zertrümmert liegt die zeit:
splitternd in tausend farben

zertrümmert liegt die zeit:
umarme mich
liebste
dass ich deine haut spüre
an meiner haut
dass wir genießen
diese handvoll zeit
die uns allein gehört

unzertrümmerbar

shattered now lies time

shattered now lies time:
it is not for you and me
to pick up the shivers yet
and piece her back together

shattered now lies time:
splintered in a thousand hues

shattered now lies time:
embrace me
love
that I feel your skin
against my skin
that we enjoy
this handful of time
that is for us alone

unshatterrable

wie xerxes

wie xerxes
das meer auspeitschte
nach einer verlorenen schlacht

so möchte ich die zeit
auspeitschen
nach einer verlorenen liebe

doch wir beide
xerxes und ich
müssen erfahren:

das meer
&
die zeit
sie sind stärker als wir
unempfindlich
gegen schmerz & schrei

so bleibt alles wie es war

verlorene schlachten
verlorene liebe

die zeiten ungesühnt

as xerxes

as xerxes
lashed out at the tide
for the losing of a battle

so I long to lash
out at time
for the losing of a love

still we two
xerxes and I
must come to learn:

time
&
tide
are stronger still than we
insensible
to wound & wail

so all remains as it was

loss of battles
loss of love

time's hand injurious

das auge der zeit

in einem alten buch
verstaubt
    /
      vergilbt
        /
          vergessen
zwischen altem zeug
briefen
   /
      versteinerten muscheln
         /
           münzen
die zeit ist darüber gekrochen wie
eine krätzige schildkröte -

wie lange ist's her
        wie lange?
mein blick fällt auf die telefonnummer
auf der rückseite des buchs
hingekritzelt hastig & in kugelschreiberblau
765 361 4244
durchgestrichen mit knalligem rot
annabelle –

the eye of time

in a dusty book
forlorn
        /
            forgot
                /
                    forsaken
among dusty old
papers
        /
            fossiled seashells
                    /
                        coins
that time had overrun like
a crusty old tortoise –

how long's it been there
                    how long?
my eye falls on the telephone number
on the back of the book
scribbled in haste & in ballpoint blue
765 361 4244
scratched out again in brilliant red
annabelle --

nebelhaft schält sie sich
aus meiner erinnerung wie aus seidenpapier
eine zufallsbekanntschaft war es
ein schönes spiel für eine nacht
im flugzeug saßen wir nebeneinander
auf dem rückflug von san francisco
nach frankfurt am main
eine lange zeit
zu lange
um nur nebeneinander zu sitzen
na ihr wisst schon
es gibt dinge
die geschehen
weil sie geschehen müssen
wir haben keine wahl
ausgeliefert
    /
       gefesselt sind wir
an einen willen
    den wir nicht kennen
        nie kennen werden:
ich hatte sie längst vergessen
abgelegt in der zeit
abgespeichert in meinen grauen zellen
       /
        unauffindbar

nebulously unwrapping herself
from my memory as from tissue paper
a chance encounter was it
a lovely one night stand
on an plane sitting next to one another
on the return flight from san francisco
to frankfurt/main
a long time
too long
just sitting next to one another
well you know already
there are things
that happen
for happen they must
we have no choice
delivered
          /
             shackled are we
   to an end
           we know not of
                      will never know:
   I'd forgotten her long since
   lain aside in time
   filed at the back of my grayest cells
                       /
                      uncatalogued

wenn nicht
ja diese telefonnummer gewesen wäre
die plötzlich vor mir
zu flimmern beginnt
sieben sechs fünf
       drei sechs eins
              vier zwei
                     vier vier:
sie tanzen & torkeln unter dem roten strich
verwirbeln zu einer spirale
aus der mich ein auge anblickt
zeitenlos tief
lockend
     /
        begehrend
           /
              verlangend

blut & lust

:

das auge der zeit

unless
this telephone number was meant to be
suddenly flickering
to life before me
seven six five
        three six one
                four two
                        four four:
twisting & turning beneath that red scratch
and swirling in a spiral
out of which an eye stares back
timeless deep
beckoning
        /
            desiring
                    /
                        demanding
blood & lust

:

that eye of time

was aber ist die zeit in der liebe?

als ich sie kennenlernte
war sie fünfzehn
ich war siebzehn

       sie hatte
einen unverschämt roten mund
wie eingefärbt von ihrem
eigenen blut
schmale hüften
in denen
ihre schosshaare schwammen
wie ein schwalbennest
              ihre brüste
waren erst im kommen
zu klein zum spielen
zum küssen allenfalls
ihre brustspitzen immerhin:
wie rote spargelspitzen
wuchsen sie hervor

sie liebte meine haut
leckte an meinen fingern
biss mich in nase & ohrläppchen
schenkte mir ein gedicht der kaga no chiyu
um mein brunnenseil
rankt eine winde sich -
gib mir wasser, freund!
ihre zierliche schrift:
musiknoten
die von einem blatt herunterkullerten

but what is time in love?

when I knew her first
she was fifteen
I was seventeen

                    she had
an unabashed red mouth
as if rouged from her
own blood
narrow hips
in between
the snarled hairs swelling
like a swallows-nest
                       her breasts
were still in coming
too small to fondle
to kiss in any event
her breast-tips nevertheless:
like red asparagus-tips
poised in bursting forth

she loved my skin
licking at my fingers
nibbling my nose & earlobes
giving me a poem of kaga no chiyu
about my well-rope
fast entwined, a vine --
give me water, friend!
her graceful scrawl:
like musical notes
spilling out across the page

sie lachte gern
sie lachte wenn sie kam
sie lachte wenn sie ging
ein lautes
übermütiges
lüsternes lachen -

irgendwann ging es auseinander
warum:
ich weiß es nicht
nach mir kam ihr klavierlehrer
dann ein bauunternehmer
ein apotheker
                /
                        ein modeschöpfer –
ihre liebhaber heftete sie
auf eine schnur
wie tibetanische gebetsfahnen

schließlich verlor ich sie aus den augen
vielleicht war sie auch ausgewandert
nach australien –

                        BIS
eines tages
zweiundvierzig jahre später
es ist dieselbe stimme
es ist dasselbe lachen
das mir entgegenrollt
durchs telefon
"ich bin auf der durchreise und
da dachte ich ..."

she laughed a lot
she laughed when she came
she laughed when she went
a loud
over-vivacious
lascivious laugh –

sometime or other it fell apart
why:
I've no idea
after me came her piano teacher
then a building contractor
a pharmacist
                    /
                    a fashion designer –
she strung her lovers
on a string
like tibetan prayer flags

eventually I lost sight of her
who knows maybe she had moved down under
to australia --

                    TILL
one day
forty-two years later
it's the same voice
it's the same laugh
that spills out over
the telephone
"I was just passing through and
and so I thought…"

und alles ist wie früher
ihre lippen
ihre lust auf meine haut
ihre spitzen schreie
wenn sie kommt und kommt
und wieder kommt
als wolle sie nie aufhören
nur ihre brüste sind größer als damals
aschgrau ihr haar
aber das ist auch schon alles
und die zweiundvierzig jahre
seither

verschluckt von der zeit

als hätte es sie nie gegeben

and everything was as it was
her lips
her lust for skin
her piercing screams
when she came and came
and came again
as if she'd never stop
only her breasts were larger than before
her hair ash-gray
however that was all
and the forty-two years
since

swallowed by time

     as if they'd never passed

manchmal besucht mich die zeit

manchmal
besucht mich die zeit
sie setzt sich auf meinen schoss
küsst mich
auf mund
augen
mein geschlecht

sie sagt:
ich komme
um dich zu lieben
mit dir zu spielen
glasperlenspiele
um mit dir zu tanzen
über dem abgrund
nichts ahnst du
von dem abgrund
von der tiefe unter dir
sicher bist du
an meiner hand

vergiss dies nicht
wenn ich einmal komme
um dich mit mir zu nehmen
in die

zeitlosigkeit

sometimes time pays me a visit

sometimes
time pays me a visit
seating herself on my lap
caressing me
on my lips
my eyes
my sex

and says:
I come
but to love you
but to play you
glass-bead games
but to dance you
over the abyss
naught to fear
of the abyss
to the depths beneath
in my hands
you are safe

forget this not
when at last I come
to take you off with me
into

timelessness

für a.

flieg ich zeitig auf die zeit
weicht sie mir zurück
kehre ich mich von der zeit
hält sie mich verstrickt

was ich dichte / treibe / kann
sie ist da und bleibt gemein
nur im kuss ab und an
lässt sie mich allein

for a.

if I fly out of time with time
she gently winds me back
if I turn my back on time
she holds me in check

whatever I write / practice / preach
she's there and stays the course
only in kisses off and on
she leaves me alone

umbalsamt meine liebe bist du

umbalsamt meine liebe bist du
umtaut von frischer zeit
so hat es celan übersetzt
dieses shakespear'sche gedicht
ist nicht darin zuviel des zaubers
zuviel der poesie
zuviel des duftes
myrrhe & rosenöl
zuviel der tausendundeine nacht
sarah & esther:

nicht öffnen wollen sich
deutsche lippen leicht
bei diesen worten
umbalsamt meine liebe bist du

DOCH

dann dies:
umtaut von frischer zeit

ein schönes bild
du liebst
im tau
in frischer zeit

verfalltag: ewigkeit

fast embalm'st my love art thou

fast embalm'st my love art thou
endew'd by time refresh'd
so celan rendered
these shakespearean lines
yet I could argue far too fanciful
far too lyrical
far too odors-sweet
myrrh & frankincense
far too thousand-and-one nights
sarah & esther:

never so lightly shall
such words as these
fall on modern lips
fast embalm'st my love art thou

STILL

there's this:
endew'd by time refresh'd

lovely image
to love
in dew
by time refreshed

reckoning-day: eternity

wenn es die zeit
      nicht gäbe

gäbe es auch nicht
dich & mich

wenn es die zeit nicht gäbe
gäbe es auch nicht:
unsere liebe

&

auch nicht: den tod unserer liebe

so ist alles in der zeit

leben
lieben
&
der liebe
tod

if it were not
for time

there would not be
you & me

if it were not for time
there would not be
our love

&

not too: the death of our love

so is all with time

life
love
&
our love's
death

zeitenebbe / zeitenflut

es gibt tage
da zieht sich
die zeit von mir zurück
wie das meer
sich zurückzieht vom land
bei ebbe
:
legt frei
muscheln
sand
treibholz
rostiges zeug
:
fräst in den schlick
rinnen
&
risse
in denen das wasser
sickert
wie dünnes blut
mein blut

nackt
&
elend fühle ich mich dann
ausgeliefert
dem licht
schutzlos die augen
                                    BIS
mich das meer
wieder einholt/überflutet
die zeit zurückkehrt
in mich
zu neuem leben
die liebe neu

ebb-time / flood-time

there are days
that ebb the time
itself away from me
as the sea
itself ebbs from the land
low tide
:
leaving behind
seashells
sand
driftwood
rusted junk
:
fast in the slime
trenches
&
troughs
through which the water
trickles
like diluted blood
my blood

naked
&
wretched feel I then
delivered
eyes defenseless
to the light

                              TILL

again the sea
sweeps me up/upon its flood
time again returns
in me
to live anew
to love anew

vergangen sind die jahre

vergangen sind die jahre
& mit ihr die zeit

ausgelöscht ist sie
wie die kreidezeichen auf der schiefertafel

verweht wie die spur des skorpions
im sand über die
der wind gegangen ist
keinen schatten wirft sie
gab es sie je?

nichts bleibt von ihr
nichts zeugt von ihr

wäre da nicht die narbe
die du geschlagen
vor zeiten

vanished are the years

vanished are the years
& with them time

erased is she
like chalk wiped clean from off the slate

scattered as a scorpion's trace
in sand over which
the wind has swept
not a shadow casts she
did she ever?

nothing left of her
nothing lives of her

were it not for the wound
that you once struck
ere times

wie wer ihr entrinnen wollte

wie wer zum haus
sie tragen wollte
gleich einem korb früchte
die zeit

wie wer sie trinken
wollte gleich wein
aus irdenem becher
die zeit

wie wer lieben wollte
in ihrem schatten
des mittags
die zeit

wie wer ihr
entrinnen wollte
gleich ein baum der axt
die zeit

as one from her would flee

as one to home
bears her
like basketsful of fruit
time

as one like wine
drinks her
as from an earthen cup
time

as one would love
in its shadow
the noon-tide sun
time

as one from her
would flee
like a tree the axe
time

liebesgedicht: das rot der zeit

die zeit ist zwischen uns
wie eine kostbare perle
eingefasst vom weichen/federnden
fleisch unserer körper

perlmuttblau
die schale
muschelkalkweiß

                manchmal
öffnet sie sich
einen spalt:
wasser dringt ein
schwebeteilchen
umströmen uns

schwerelos sinken wir
ins rot
der zeit

love poem: the flush of time

time is between us
like a precious pearl
encompassed by the gentle/feathered
flesh of our bodies

mother-of-pearl blue
the shell
musselchalk white

                    now and then
opening up
a crack:
waters rushing
flotsam flooding in
engulfing us

weightless sink we
in the flush
of time

tempus docet

früher
am morgen
   nach getaner liebe
habe ich sie fortgeschickt

heute
am morgen
   nach getaner liebe
bleiben sie bei mir

was ist es
das anders geworden ist
mit mir

seither?

tempus docet

once
come morning
  after making love
I'd push them from me

now
come morning
  after making love
they stay by me

what is it
that has otherwise become
of me

since?

ZEIT

morgen. mittag. abend.

mai. november.

das leben fließt dahin
wie ein träger fluss

ODER

ein sturzbach ist es
            der dich niederreißt
in seine strudel
&
untiefen

freundschaften zerbrechen
träume versteinern
die hoffnung: ein rostiger nagel in der wand
liebe: zu asche wird sie zu asche

die straßen
durch die du gegangen bist:
sie sind nicht mehr
und auch nicht:

TIME

morning. noon. night.

may. november.

life flowing thither
like a lazy stream

OR

a maelstrom is it
dragging you down
in its swirl
&
fathomless deep

friendships shatter
dreams turn stone
hope: no more than a rusty nail in the wall
love: ashes to ashes dust to dust

the streets
through which you've gone:
are since no more
and gone too:

die tür
die du so oft durchschritten

am ufer stehe ich
schaue in das spiel der wellen
wie sie sich auftürmen & zusammenbrechen
gezeiten der zeit

was bleibt:

der wechsel der dinge
&
die sehnsucht die sehnsucht

die in dir blutet
eine wunde
die nicht verheilt

rgm

the door
through which you so often stepped

upon the bank I stand
staring at the play of the waves
how they tower & fall to break together
on the tidings of time

what's left:

the turn of things
&
the yearning the yearning

that bleeds within
a wound
that never heals

RALPH GÜNTHER MOHNNAU was born in 1937 in the town of Bad Kreuznach, Germany. First poems and articles appeared at age 14, and an interest in poetry, painting and ballet was followed by studies in English and Romance languages, with degrees in Law and Philosophy from the Universities of Mainz, Freiburg and the Paris Sorbonne. His foreign studies have taken him to Greece, Egypt, the United States and the Canary Islands, crediting personal encounters with Martin Heidegger, Alain Robbe-Grillet, Charles Bukowski, Joan Miró, and John Cage as significant influences on his creative work.

All told, he has published more than 60 volumes of his works, many of which have been translated into English, French, Spanish, Catalan, and Japanese. His poems have been collected under the titles: *RED CORPUSCLES, ANTI-BODIES, GAMMA-RAYS* and *SOWING NIGHTSHADE IN THE WASTELANDS OF CITIES*. He has written a novel, *DANCE OF THE CONDOR*, and translated Akenaten's *THE SONG OF THE SUN*, and *THE LOVE POEMS* of Sappho.

Beyond poetry, his creative passions extend to musical theatre and opera. He has written several libretti -- *CAROLINE* (score composed by Michael Obst, Weimar), *WENN DIE ZEIT ÜBER DIE UFER TRITT* (If Time Overflow the Banks, for the Munich Biennale, score by Vladimir Tarnopolski), and *JENSEITS DER SCHATTEN* (*Beyond the Shadows*, for the Beethoven Festival in Bonn, score by Vladimir Tarnopolski, Moscow). His rock opera *H-OR, THE RAINBOW JUMPERS* (score by Matthias Raue), had its premiere at the Ohio Theatre off-Broadway in 1985, directed by OBIE-Award winner Manuel Lütgenhorst. A dramatic work, *CRY OF THE MANTIS* has been mounted in Paris, Vienna, Frankfurt, and at Seven Stages/Atlanta in 1990, director/designer Christopher Martin, music by Matthias Raue.

Ralph Günther Mohnnau lives and works in Frankfurt and Ibiza (Balearic Islands, Spain).

CHRISTOPHER MARTIN is a director/designer and composer, the Founding Artistic Director of Classic Stage Company in New York where he mounted a hundred productions over the company's first eighteen years, frequently appearing as an actor. Since 1985, his work has taken him to National and State Theatres across Europe and the Far East. As a translator, he has received a Pulitzer Prize nomination (with Daniel Woker) for the Heiner Müller text of Robert Wilson's THE CIVIL WARS (American Repertory Theatre), and the National Theatre Translation Fund Award for versions of German playwright Botho Strauss. A designated translator of the plays of Federico Garcia Lorca, he has also rendered Rostand's rhymed verse CYRANO DE BERGERAC, and plays by Roger Planchon, Moliére, Strindberg, Büchner, Wedekind, and Dürrenmatt. He is currently at work on a series of crime novels.

INDEX

...and thus hailed: a life steeped in time

...that is time spilling across your tongue

...out of the lap of my beloved lapping time

Printed in the United States
By Bookmasters